Slant

Linda Black

Slant

Shearsman Books

First published in the United Kingdom in 2016 by
Shearsman Books
50 Westons Hill Drive
Emersons Green
BRISTOL
BS16 7DF

Shearsman Books Ltd Registered Office
30–31 St. James Place, Mangotsfield, Bristol BS16 9JB
(this address not for correspondence)

www.shearsman.com

ISBN 978-1-84861-468-0

ACKNOWLEDGEMENTS
My thanks to the Editors of the following journals in which some of these
poems were previously published: *The Wolf, Shearsman, Magma, Brand, Tears
in the Fence*, and the online journals *Horizon Review, Litter* and *Interlitq* (The
International Literary Quarterly). 'A Poem & a Bead' was commended in
a *Poetry London* Competition and appeared on their website. 'Green' was
commissioned by Roddy Lumsden. 'This is not her' appeared in the anthology
Drifting Down the Lane (Moon & Mountain, 2013, edited by Harriette Lawler
and Agnes Marton). Some poems were previously published in the pamphlet
The beating of wings (Linda Black, 2006, Hearing Eye) and in the anthologies,
This Little Stretch of Life (Hearing Eye, 2006, edited by Karen Green & Mimi
Khalvati) and *I am 20 people!* (Enitharmon, 2007, edited by Mimi Khalvati
& Stephen Knight).

My thanks also to Mimi Khalvati, Claire Crowther and Lucy Hamilton for
their feedback, and of course to Tony Frazer for publishing the book.

Contents

She will advise her neighbour to plant aubrietia

The earth is dry & banked   here & there
the sods are separate congealed with clay
She kneels cupping soil with her own bare hands
smooths / sifts / rearranges as though she has a plan
to return to Oh how the earth ascends!
(which requires a little explanation) like rocks
above a canyon   cantilevered   held
as if by air alone

And here now in the background
is her neighbour   emerging
from a side door   How exactly will she explain
to another   what she can't to herself?

Ask how she is

Say: how is it with you? expect her
            to sigh to shift to stir

                A match (unlit)
falls to the floor it lands
            poised between boards with another
she prises it out

            In the small of her back
                a vertebra
clicks into place   shoulders
                        melt fractionally
            as imperceptible
as a snowflake's demise She is focused
            on the gladioli:
a tall / stark / rigid stem   rooted
            where it ought not cannot No sooner *that*
than the memory of last night's
            sudden windfall – a wad of notes
in a pocket – her pocket? &
            who was it trying to take it from her?
                Sigh all those birds so
perfect up there – lost
                in an avalanche
                – graphic speedy
incomplete
                taking with it . . .

She is elsewhere

A thought sticks
almost as soon as it has begun
& as she walks

Her coat sufficiently drab & verging
on threadbare scrapes the length
of the pavement *swish swish*

We are not in France though it could be . . .
enters a walled garden butterflies crickets
a path through a wild meadow

Yesterday she had walked
around an abandoned quarry passable
routes through rock a fireplace

Carved in a rock face the remains
of a fire rough-earth loose-earth dry-dirt
dirt where dirt should be

A lava lamp

Settles   a coat (forsaken)
hangs – when she checks it
moths fly out   In the hallway
a child is harnessed   whose teeth
are sharp as any animals (the child
she was lay on the kitchen table)

As she rises wall responds: *steady I am*
in my sloping ways   smoothed & primed & lofty
in my inclination   & so I steady her
I through whose heights she passes   pauses . . .
rendering (me) rending . . . a shell
a coldly tenement . . .

Meanwhile   she baits moths in traps
releasing pheromones

Skip stairs
three at a time
jump ship . . .

She walks for days

Up & down stairs   in & out
the washing machine   has become
where she is   where the moon got her
She has nowhere   goes by foot
tripping over her own   worse for wear
explains nothing   doesn't admit   she is not
of that faith   It is many years ago now
she turned   & walked away   no thought
from her own good   someone else's
consequence   & the madman   inside
where ten pinafores hang

What a clever thing   she just did
she calls people   she hasn't seen for years
she is proud!   When she leaves
the first time is seriously threatened
bump bump bump   headfirst
on the back wheels   As no one has told
& no one is   so all day   this thing
from out of her   propped upright

A saviour in a soft jumper
or her sister's skin   she has no clear
picture   apart from preferring
long fingers   In that seated posture
did Keats have long fingers?   a balanced

book a crossed knee *but* . . .
she corrects herself One hand is
one head was then retracts
too much of a put down
a Regency chair but it could be

The air comes up against her
  has extremities both she covets
she covets both Under the carpet
looking out   all she can see
is space She does not want a box
gathering what she incorporates
would anyone? She stays inside
hers sometimes venting

All day it puzzles her
  from dwelling How exactly?
a slight small & precise
remembered from life to another
what she couldn't herself   the same words
repeated in the future   very slight
changes not circles exactly

A good few years ago he told her
  like a beam she imagined a searchlight
from out of the top of her head   then
about the needles   a pincushion
he said   it must have been
unbearable So many objects
shedding light

Turn to where there is no light
check she is here She must not
run pell-mell along the side
of the hearth where the edge
meets the craved way Today
she looks to the sky thinking
to be someone else
A visitor say

Where dazed people live shy
to the bare branches shall go somewhere
back to the bare ground Could it be
this is the very same jug
or distant relative? A chair
transposed no regard for age
or time Passes quicker
Shall not notice
what her eyes see

Something flimsy
of little input not cracked up
to be really very fragile
wrapped in cellophane distanced
from the swing the wood
the unnecessary detail

Scene 1: In the hallway

—tin pink flower heads
on green stick stalks   fifty million
round the light switch   Above a doorway
second right   an arch   revealed
whilst decorating   a recess
not quite big enough   A fallen coat
seeding fluff & coppers   dribs
of tissue   a pocket
reminder – soap   nappies   a trivial
box of matches
A reversible garment
waterproofed
on one side

Encumbered   she checks   tries
to make haste   to leave   to leave
behind   A look . . . *bemuse / behold / bewilder* . . . inkling
of an elsewhere mind   all knowledge
erased   She with the eyes
in the back of her head – call it
intuition . . . *call it summons it*   standing
halfway   along the hallway   that   place
of passages   facing out   no intention
of taking   a different route   An innocent . . .
follow her follow   as small piles
reassemble   on each stair   fronds
recoil   water inverts   sucked up the drainpipe: the bed's
unmaking   retractable

like a metal rule
a dragon's
intake of fire

A knowing wall   a window's
back & future   – a slice
down the middle   So many
changes of clothing   a fringe snipped so many times   *there she goes* . . .
with an open heart – a figment   chewing
on liquorice comfort   Fortnightly
the insurance man calls   milkman Thursdays savings
in the post office   green-shield stamps   – taut like elastic
ready to fire   Forwards
to go back   to end up
wrong footed (heels or flats?)   – a question
of where the weight falls
hindsight
heretofore . . .

a small occasion   at the rate
a finger nail grows   a scar
takes to fade   the skin's response
to a too hot handle   cools
under running water   Inborn   Towards
creation . . .   *back & back & back* to the day   a mirror
fell from the wall onto a rug   where
all childhood played   – but she'd gone in that split
crescendo   to answer the call
of a neighbour: familiarity
in the back streets
tar in the gutter . . .
from   whence   she   came . . .

She takes herself out of herself

Little gregarious footings

holds   falls   takes a-back

Who is she from?   *bairn-breech cairn-borne   spittle & clay*

The matter is nebulous   the climate

untenable   *lock-spawn   milk-spurn   bile-bred   flay*

She gets out: *crumb-path   snake-slaw   Betty's café*

One carves from one an other   *whip-spore   egg-mire   bird-brunt   fray*

Caring comes away   *foal-drift   turn-fork   brawn & bray*

Goodbye   *split-dew   flesh-core   coal-mist   prey*

Goodbye   *gristle & snatch*

cackle & knuckle   *caw caw candy*

Verbiage

Speech proves little lasting
– thought becomes a barrier
into which she runs

In the outside world
a tree whose branches won't obscure
the evening's light

She does return
years later skin pale as dew on its way
to old   *tap tap*

Green-swirls carpet
tentatively knocking   – is it enough
to imagine satisfaction?

Take first the landing
each transitional board each gap
each cautionary nail

Veering towards the intangible
– it is almost as if she were
a magnet attracting the unnecessary

Seen from the past

Reel to the moment
Briar & firstborn
Bird-song & beetle
Petal & nettle

Careless & cloven
Rushing & raw
Hears her a twinkle
Clamber & claw

Saddle & shutter
Prickle & thimble
Mix & mock
Fail-sooth & fallow
Holed in the ginnel
Hook line & sink her

Slip-shod & scupper
Nurture or flaw
Kick & lock
Parch-peel & hallow
Bolder than bramble
Whip-bode all winter

Cold & alluded
Small bits stolen
Cornered & brooding
Wind-wept colluded

Lip-spat exuded
Torn-from excluded
Itch-pitch intruding
Scolded & sore

Under the hedgerow
Wasps where the seeds sow
Down by the dust roots
Pig in the hen-hutch
Clay-ring & tallow

All of a shamble
Pawed where the worms glow
Lost in the bind shoots
Witch in the reed-patch
Maid of the marrow

Hers is a pin-prick
Hold her & mould her
Fine coils & flutter
Kind-heart & keep her

Tear-hole & charm trick
Seek her & fold her
Soft sheets & butter
Safe from the gutter

Indelible

A tangle of pipe   a length

of coiled wire   daisy threads

squealing   *flick-snick   dead-sedge*

beads   hanging

on   *neck-slit   egg-snap*

old rope

over wound   *eye-dread   dry-bred*

cruel work   replica (intimate)

transformations

Stipulate   a body

to work on   *pick-pounce*

taut   prayed for   *nut-splat   cold-sack*

is it not

a long way from home?

This is not her

Whose shadow dances   in the eves
assumes a pirouette   scaling the heights
of a cathedral   Chartres say or Rouen   tall
as a mountain's peak – *up   up   & up*
spawning the wings of an angel
an Esmeralda   in the belfry
acquitted of all sin

Whose persecutor   lures her
to extremes   whose psyche   is slaked
but will not relinquish

From her perspective (outside of all this)
a door bars the way   a door
as thick as stone   built on the deaths
of a thousand prophets

hailstone   rock-strewn   gravestone   gravel . . .

The insistence of air the ringing
inside an ear of intent

What can she do who only observes?

Never a (moment)

To clarify (the many hours up until)
       drizzle outside
inside   the weather sniffles closes
       in claws
a rose off a wall – it sprawls
       prostrate about it
a misplaced warmth
            chilling
       for the time of year

      Stacked prints slide
on bowed shelves tapers
      lie limp Dutch mordant
        crystallises
in brown glass jars Images
      etched
return to the copper coated
      in Vaseline
        layered in tissue

She stoops (our lady our lass)
       then – from the garden
– an arc a line
       with pegs attached a brightness
cast She rises
       but the moment's past

Beauty

She thinks
    cannot be stolen   In this
she is uncertain   By the light
    of all that is unforetold (she vows)
I shall not be forsaken   *I shall not!*
    Had she not lived once
in a house with uneven floors?   Was she
    not swarthy?   She could
      have gone on . . .

Things went on
for some time . . .   & so it came to pass
    on a day made entirely
of such sweet soft remembrances
    of the kind she long
longed to experience   that
    which she least
(were she to have thought of it)
    expected . . .

. . . A *somebody* : a personage
a bon-vivant? a raconteur?
    passing by *her* gate
(or where a gate would have been
    had there been one)
    Suddenly *this*!

Earth's spread

—legend
quickens   outward
inward to the fine grit
sand   sieved & airborne
scuffs the surface
into drills   blows in
three wishes   bows out
definition   beaten by whether . . .
O fragile web!

Far far lower:
fossils   scavengers   bones
stilled   unsettled   & up / out there
a dandelion clock

Be it alive

As bulbs below a tree
burst through grass
naturalize this thought
had but a small start

Seeded & watered its roots
splay scour for substance
surface to sandstorms
peppery & wired

Excusing herself she leaves the room
her forehead brain ears & eyes
accompanying   assailed
by all & sundry

Blank walls of porous material
so much the better for its weariness
its worn away looks
anticipate her return

At this point   nearing Spring
the pushing through
is delicate unassuming

Small things in the soil

A crispen leaf a cleft shell a corridor

of earthworm growth

clipped (she prunes)   cut

& the more will grow

Examine the ashes – a clenched carapace

a curled wood-louse   a bit

of a dead fly –

hoe / layer / supplant   disturb

roots rodents   sever clumps

In the scheme of things . . .

rhizomes wrapped in newspaper

scab / knot / knuckle

          defiguration

   not by any means

immaterial – skin

of the earth

under the nails

The composition of soil

its exhumation   its seepages

harbinger

of the wriggling   malleable

in its nature   in variations   & all its various

properties   the country over   wide

& deep-set   endless

in its constitution   wayward dense & undulating

slip-soil   slow-soil   sacred-soil   soft

ash & bone   embellished

in formation   foundation

of all that is natural   its defiance

of ever ending

*

through the window she *sees* the garden

sharp & forthright   earth-patch   life-patch   lease

of life —*sees* the ascending —*sees* the plum tree   birds

accumulate amongst its dead branches   source

of life   wall trellis pergola   urn

of earth (down to)   athwart

in feign protection

In this land

Of living proportions

Accruement & dispersal   what need

Of this amounting   *seed-welt / wold-warp / spittle*

That gathering   of the un-together

Each laden branch

Wilting   *soul-slew / catch-curl / forbears / fever*

All of which is wounding

To the already wounded   *cross-axe / hatch-bow / word-weld / dagger*

You ask how I know   I speak

Of institutions   failings of mores   personalities

Whose props may (as well)

Be the dunces-cap   the cane   the wielding

Of liturgies   *whip-gall / snake-lore / bird-creed / rebel*

And so on   locking up   repetition   the culling

Of what could be   *switch-block / bone-metal / spindle-finger / meddle*

As we would have it   as we thought

We knew it   *nay not   ne'er*

Green

O joke! O spring!

elm-haw & ash-row wan-thorn & elder

cone & conniver   dun for

olive   alive to verdigris

O penstemon!   lush

on the verge   So she delves:

wood for the wainscot

briar for the bower   *vary-gate vale-strim   grain-shire prickle /*
brine-elf & bodkin

soldiers on   (khaki the mettle)

Turf folds the velvet glen   (gain says the merry men)

sleek & contiguous

fine-stem   frond-weed   roiled-fern   forest

-

Forest sweep   Forest flair

Weep for the forest   *brush & mire   girth & cradle*

Swaddle the forest

Grizedale   Whinfell   Ashclyst   Kinver

furnish   wreath & garnish

brittle the swale   sward & dale

Shroud the forest　　Skein the forest dell

Bowthorp　　Belvoire　　Fortingale

ˎ

Maidens frolic the land's breath

trip   to the bare wold　　*covert & coppice　dingle & thicket*

Swain & warrior

gamble   o'er fields of mottled blood

Swoon for the pasture　　Slain for the blunder　　*whence war & wander*

render   the shire's end

fallow & tree-less

ˎ

O celandine ! O lesser-wort!

foiled in the snicket

O rolling hills!　　fold the heart's desire　　breach

the sleeve's declivity　　evergreen

& hem-locked

Fruit of the cleft　　Foist of the jest

bold/en the leaf　　*mould　weald & frith*

a-top the gatepost

Over the crest

I know now what a tinkling brook is

(From the diaries of Gerard Manley Hopkins)

Suppose *three* (as there often are)   in the confusion

    of the already folded   morning-bright

& every-way: A high field   a hedge   a tree

    (the country is full of fine trees) the lisp

of a swallows wing – the link between

    now / then / even-yet   in one instance

flies flush & swift: Rib-stem end-shoot   leaf-star

    (how many you could not tell) – much turns

on the broadness of a leaf   The horizon

    balances its blue rim   pewits wheel & tumble

as they are said to do . . . *but not for this liquidity* . . .

    dips & waves foreshortening

so differenced in brightness & opacity   slanting

    beyond the skyline . . . a thread

in smooth rivers . . . fair or fine or cold   all lodged

    one with another . . . & the want

to carve out   Midway a pair of elms: by taking a few steps

    one could pass the further

behind the nearer: Whichever of the two sides

    you slide the hinder tree   rib & spandrel

chip the sky & where their waved edge

turns downward   they gleam & blaze   remarkably so

& clear   bluebell / primrose / campion – the two latter

or two former matching gracefully   but not so well

the three: hemlock in clouds of bloom

lap-waved shadow-stroked   scarcely

expressing form: the relief of green – light

in the close grass converging

& diverging   suggests rose in a recondite way

So it looks – through all the rack

the parts seem to close as if it were a translation

of rose or rose in another key

The seven lamps

(after Ruskin)

L ook abroad into the landscape
so bent & fragmentary – the flowing river
its pebbled bed Out of the kneaded fields
concretions of lime & clay loosely struck
small habitations alike without difference built
in the hope of leaving lived in the hope
of forgetting   vanquished
in the hanging thickets of hillsides
Ribands occur frequently in arabesques flitting
hither & thither among the fixed forms
apologetic drifting into what they will
no beginning nor end – no strength no skeleton
no make no will of their own only
flutter Let the flowers come loose . . .

L ong low lines rise soon to be lifted
& wildly broken Far-reaching ridges
rend their rude & changeful ways
those ever springing flowers – conquerors
of forgetfulness – more precious in memories
than in the renewing The pavement rises
& falls arches nod westward & sink not one
of like height These inclinations:
the accidental leaning the curious incidence
of distortion – differences

in which they are lightly engaged
exquisite delicacies of change tallied
to a hair's breath – have grace
about them a sensation in every inch

The goodly street: many a pretty beading
& graceful bracket the warm sleep of sunshine
upon it Count its stones set watches about it
where it loosens bind it with iron stay it with timber
tenderly When the pitcher is rested the breath
drawn deeply what pause so sweet? In the declivity
of a hill between the heights of stories serenity
holds out its strong arm But if to stone be added
intervals arched & trefoiled   hangings of
purple & scarlet   taches of brass sockets
of silver twisted with tracery & starry light charged
with wild fancy I would fain introduce
a narrow door a foot-worn sill a hearth
of mica slate a steel grate a polished fender

Rests and monotones settle at first
contentedly in the recess of a rose window
Under the dark quietness blunt-edged rosettes
neither bend nor grow This interval – an arborescence
a candied conglomerate through which we pass –
not that it is indolence or the feebleness
of childhood breaks away the bark

in noble rents A life of custom & accident
losing sight animates puts gestures
in clouds voices into rock A double creature
feigned or unfeigned speaks
what we do not mean like the flow
of a lava stream languid settling
crusted over with idle matter

In the discontented present a certain deception
the root unseen spreads like a winding sheet
irregular stems of ivy run up hollows – a falling tendril
the creeping thing The very quietness of nature
restless against a dead wall In the chasms & rents
of rocks the wind has no power ridge rising over ridge
in absolute bluntness Cut & crush
what you will More has been gleaned out of
desolation At the meeting of the dark streets
the spire with its pinnacles winged griffins stirring
within the tympanum – in gloomy rows disquieted walls
shells of splintered wood foundationless
tottering A desecrated landscape – walk
in sorrow rend it lightly & pour out its ashes

I once thought that which I could not love
diminished more than it increased –
the snow the vapour & the stormy wind
cold interiors of cathedrals bordered

by the impure in all the meanest
& most familiar forms – I could not bear
one drifting shower! Details
even to the cracks in stones rise
strange & impatient chrystallised
as with hoar frost   memoranda
thrown together – I cannot answer
for accuracy There is something
to be grateful for even weeds
are useful that grow on a bank of sand

The hours of life as if measured
    by the angel's rod let them be gathered
well together in woods & thickets
in plains cliffs & waters
The setting forth of magnitude beheld
with never ceasing delight   infinity of fair form
fairest in the quiet lake the surface
wide bold & unbroken light
blossoming upon it A great entail
So again it sails! The face of a wall is
as nothing – is infinite! – its edge
against the sky like a horizon the eye drawn
to its terminal lines Time and storm
set their wild signatures

The odd daisy

That signpost you can't read
        till closer (near / far / eternity)
                wooden of course at the end
of a country lane: a country house
        admission free perhaps
                a small donation
loose change in the pocket – the day ahead
        encouraging weather or just
                that it is not yet late

How a house echoes: tall ceilings
        polished floors drapery
                hanging in folds the many ways
to open a door – attending
        to the little fascinations On the lawn
                which would be long
undulating   well cared for
        there may be the odd daisy
                a small patch
to stop & stoop at – nothing dramatic
        an angel slightly crumbling
                a wing a posy of stone

With much to see
        the eyes tire & then
                a kind of glazing over
– a pause – the time it takes
        to tie a shoelace   the chink / scrape / slur
                of a drawing pin
embedded in the sole: exactly that
        though I would have liked
                that there were a sundial

Bells

I see them upright
        on their stems – how intense
the blue! – paler
        on the inside Soon
their light blunders   *tick tick*
            The grass does not know
which way to blow
        a blade   a whistle   a stain   a cut

Their heads nod
        in different directions:
fawn & fade in all
        the extraordinary air

It comes down on me
        down on me . . . white that is
            almost blue blue
            that is almost white

In the interim:

A deer or an antelope poised in the long grass

the sound of rustling as there is now

plucked startled from where it does

to where it does not belong a process

of interruption What is all this waiting for?

A bookshelf a vase of flowers (catches briefly

the sunlight) the indetermination of each bloom

A rocking horse rocks a picture hangs haphazard

on the wrong wall All that is makeshift the lid is off

in half readiness The creature thus procured

may be placed against a background posed in a room

for living (see above) a pattern of diamonds

or some such décor a focus for elaboration

on which the pencil may linger One graceful limb

(almost human) crossing gracefully at the ankle

the other Gaze tethered between two worlds

(from now on it could go many ways)

When disappointed the will is whittled away

her head skewed (an old habit) There are no details:

a little tipping over as if on the way This leaning

left Unchecked goes on leaning To be so upturned

shaken like a cellar of salt   what leaks? what remains?

onto what would she hold? her hair is thick

and her nails are very strong It could be time (untitled)

leaning moribund against her wall   She wants

nothing specific a gleaning out of shadow an alteration

of what is what was To be guided henceforth

Blossoms fall in random configurations petals

curl & fade having given   according to capabilities

only so much pleasure The power of gentle flutterings

the storm the blowing away After lines that do not twist

she longs for verse Words that by chance she reads

are like a distant flock of swallows   scattered

settled among the branches: *threnody mescal aspen*

Bowl

Contemplate this:
a dust-filled bowl – mottled depressed
          in the centre suspended
from a ceiling rose
          by chains of equal length   how a hook
traverses glass   the relentless
          beating of wings
against the sides

At table at candle – position
yourself   consider your placing
          rows & layers
centuries wide – *the more she looked*
          the more it began to fade & she
to doubt its authenticity – here
          comes an over-mantel
complete with foxing

Once it seemed
no less was above than below to the right
          than to the left   one lived held
as a yolk in an egg such *middleness*
          – bliss! – not striven for then lost
as losing is All night she searches
          for the small sun:
she dreams of pull cords
          & dimmer switches

Can I move you a little?

—the neck of a guitar (goaded to silence)
may tilt pleasing to the eye
that bothers to observe   takes measure
of the space in which what resounds
has no pitch no timbre: rests
just so far from the cupboard's edge
—well go on move it then

Each object knick-knack random possession
contained within its optimum space
becomes more so The more it takes the more
it gives   A valuable whole   a bearer of complexity
its own best friend (now we see more clearly)
neither detracts nor overshadows
as if in holy space What unseen negotiations
between the inert and the quick? What white light
emanates from the top of her head?
In which preferred arrangement
do we co-exist?

Her hair . . . her precious hair . . .
& her eyes   bless her eyes . . .

She looks around her eyes

Not into them at the way the flesh
folds surrounds   She has no gaze
& alopecia of the eyebrow   She has an eye
for that kind of thing – the skew-whiff
the out of place   She will find
what her eye avoids   the scarcely
visible – a second sight   a sigh
of sensibility   as though beauty
sadly were out of reach

A seeker of the best avoided   the skin
& rind   a fine judge this eye of hers
inside at the back   the closed eye
closets   gives up a beggar   a child
in a wheelchair   a head affectionately prodded
turning on like a clockwork nightingale:
a hail of song   indecipherable
but perfect

See a penny

Here – here I am indoors
in the afternoon I didn't eat – often

I don't & I breathe in
when people approach – it's a kind

of preparation   like the way
I clear my throat

if the phone rings   Some things
I'm good at   are second nature – I catch

the thread in the eye of a needle
every time – I made this dress:

three metres of cotton lawn buttonholes
stitched by hand I'm saving

– paper clips rubber bands
the postman drops pennies – I've filled

a small box – there's odd ones
in coat pockets claimed

from the streets eyes down a voice
telling me *pick it up* singing

catch a falling star thinly
silently Two things

I read not long ago stuck
in my mind: several mentions

of snow & the poet standing
– or waiting – or watching

for hours each time
from some different place

– a port maybe
a stationary train I think

of buying myself flowers how each day
repeats itself of aphids

on the undersides of leaves:
how the wind

whoops & sweeps tapers
like a witch's hat curling

round turrets & tall places while I
follow follow

Multiplicity

A leaf is nibbled   the nibbler is gone
I look underneath   no I see no-one

Stickle-cell   Yellow-edge   Pith-vein   Spore

A stem ends abruptly   stands like a waif
handless & headless   nothing is safe

Saw-finger   Grub-claw   Slime-rot   Vector

I thought you a beauty   then something thin
crept uninvited   under your skin

Raggedy-root   Blot-core   Lop-mass   Scavenger

A tell-tale sign   a sudden sharp snap
biting the bud   sucking the sap

Crown-rot   Cripple-leaf   Stunt-bloom   Mania

Pale mottled patches   velvet-grey mould
empty white husks   exposed & cold

Tulip-scorch   Red-thread   Fire-blight   Burn

I stalk a trail   silent & sallow
Blight o' the night   foiled in the marrow

Dithane   Hexyl   Longlast   Fester

She composes herself

Which face forewarns   which set
of mind   bone of hair   *clock-mop*
re-ordered   *swab-style ship-scape scalp-lock schism*
a fable in itself   *pud-proof mud-sooth*
engendered   not entirely
restorative outlying
the plot   *whit-blush rose-gape ghost-scrape madder*

A parable   for today's eye
lined   on the surface   *stick-spit lip-pluck slick-salve meddler*
what would she like to see
reflected   *Columbine   O shifting season!*
crow-bat   worm-tit tail-skew shadow

Within range of selection   begins
with tone   *curl-suit garb-dean tulle-pain garter*
or hearsay   or heresy
glove-shoe slip-gloss may-brief muddler

Stay   move closer
close   delectate
look at the picture   *pretty-pin coddle-tin pity-whim flounder-ling*

The slope of a hill

—what is the appeal
of leaning? trees houses people   all leaning
           in the same direction   as though
the world   were tilted   walls thin
           as tissue   a figure
so fragile   it will topple
           at the merest breath
                  . . . *tulips*
         float by   leafless
              uprooted . . .   feet
together   every few yards   measured
           it seems   by the placing of the gate posts
she jumps   – terraces – church spire
                  – village hall
         skewed   propped   one
against the other
                  . . . *sideways*   . . . *ballet legs*
         sinuous   stretched
              to their limits   resisting
         the pull
earthward   – faces   the faces
                  of women
                       are featureless   hidden
         by hand hair   the wing
of a passing bird
                  . . . *downhill   eyes*

down   York stone on London clay   a certain

conviction   the appearance

of an unknown room

. . . steadfastly

on   a compulsion . . .

. . . replica clouds   torn patches of chintz   roses roses   gloves

for thin fingers   a craving

for the taste of salt

. . . speechless

she refuses

to fly

on the other side

of plasterboard   voices

debate   prefabricate

. . . it is time

to go

. . . she slips   could slip

may well

. . . water

will not hold her   comes up

everywhere

running

behind her back   seeping

the length of a city

—pincers'

    finger and thumb

        a forefinger's

            calf and thigh

—erasure . . . *she hears kind of*

                   doesn't

stop

    to listen

        she can't

  be bothered   her legs

          do not part   her legs

            are stuck together   she is always

        like this   she lives

          like this   her hand

                constantly

    over her mouth   her mouth

              constantly

        open . . .

earnest voices . . . *this is the way*

    you hold

      your head

          hold

      your head

    the slant

of a ladder . . .

This little stretch of life

(from the letters of Elizabeth Bishop)

There are sanctuaries small melting snowdrifts
here & there – an atmosphere

easy to crawl into In one of those intervals
where all thought has ceased I am tempted

by waves the transparent sea I think my heart
beats twice a day – a very slight

ailment I've tried all approaches – aerial
& subterranean – I am mixed about

like a drop of oil on water. This place!
This pile of masonry! Accumulated

stray objects – you can get right under
clutching like a gasping mermaid

no view to be seen Have you ever
gone through caves? Things

just seep through the walls
I don't imagine anyone could hear me

howling I am one
of ten thousand or whatever it is

who are lost each year   In a minute or two
I know I shall forget   Excuse

my disconnectedness – I must go see
what everything is doing

– these things on my shoulders
are not wings

Look very closely

A twist persists   tips

its gnarled perspective   indigenous

fecund – no frills

nor backdrops   or places

to hide   what use

lament   stale toast

or a cup of lime   in order

to survive   hints

go cold   snapdragons perish

as does the skater   (ghost for the ride)

in the winter's depth

Where shall I sit?

I scan the room   scour surfaces
a sprig of rosemary   gracing

every clothed or unclothed table   where
are the spaces – is the angle of a chair

quite right its height   are there neighbours
who won't encroach   will I take

a cushion to the garden bench   see
how the grass has grown

to weed & clover   roses
succumbed to black-spot   gather

their serrated leaves   later curl-up
on the sofa   cross uncross cross my legs

how shall I arrange the pillows
to support my neck   will I lie

on my side or back pressure
on my swollen knee soon causing me

to shift my position where shall I rest
which plot of ground?

I could not say I tried: Cento

I set out bowls & plates   which become a house
make an evening   pass quickly enough
— compare it to a plateaux Sleep above
to get to other places   chopping & fitting
hair dishevelled   — no gleam & tinkle in it
— like a hand of which the arm
is not visible   Sometimes I come ready
in pieces   my face I think
is my own

How thirsty I am   still sat   meaning
to ask   — already sick of summer
It is a quiet room   & the green of the park
could be touched   I rise from the table
abruptly   Some of us scream
as the weather changes

Sources:
Peter Redgrove, John Ashbery, Marina Tsvetaeva,
Lee Harwood, Tom Raworth

We are like frail grass

We are like dust   but the wind
      does not move us   we are between
      but not among

The saucer is there   the cup of ambrosia
      on the stoop's
      narrow margin

The hellebore in the pot is there   the hedge
      clipped bare   the stake is there
      but not the breeze

When fledglings flee there is no mirth

Doubt compresses pleasure   firms the soil
      below the familiar tree
      & earth is contained

The days conflate   the shed the bench
      in need of oil
      shroud the glean of autumn

There is no hell   there are no spiders' webs

The campion lets go its spores   the life that holds us
      it is not ours
      flounders in its carapace

At the little deal table under the glare of the lamp

(from the diaries of Virginia Woolf)

My feeling is half moonshine I am trying to tell
whatever self it is cast shade upon me An odd thing

the human mind infinitely shying at shadows
– a little strip of pavement over an abyss Here I sit

Like a lantern in the middle of a field
my light goes up in darkness I think too much

of whys & wherefores can't settle
as I should I am twenty people! I thought

I was becoming more myself – here I am
chained to my rock one touch of red

in the cheek the machinery
a little cumbrous a cloud in my head I should

notice everything the phrase for it coming
the moment after These mists of spirit

have other causes: the shut up house
dust sheets on the chairs the least interesting of rooms

the compromise like little sips
thin as a March glaze on a pool I took a vow

I'd say what I thought think myself
infallible & so I write nonsense

that life mayn't be wasted   The windows
fidget at their fastenings   I feel now & then

a tug to vision the little owl calling
Yesterday the river burst its banks   My mind

works in idleness   – I am stuffed with ideas!
– feel I can use up everything

I have ever thought   The soul swims
from one lighted room to another

Last night I looked at the meadow – trees
flinging about   such a weight of leaves

every brandish seemed the end   I do not
love my kind – I let them break on me

like dirty raindrops   dry little shapes
floating past   second selves obscure & odd

Never mind – arrange what pieces come your way live
entirely in it   & come to the surface

obscurely   I can float everything off now:
a crowd a weight a confusion in the mind   a sense

of my own strangeness: those mountain clouds
a small stone   the fall of a flower (she too feels wonder)

Here's my interesting thing   & no quiet
solid table on which to put it

A fence   An arboretum

Plain pleasure   fixated
on the rekindling
of a bench   I shall scrub   the more
to petrify   Moss
shall be disturbed   most cloying
of its kind   & when you
are gone
I shall not miss you

I lie   I steal   I perpetuate – neither
one shall flower   if I
has my way

Now I have an end
to return to   Here at the boundary
I shall set   my confluence
ne'er   to call it home

Into the white

My person   my fiend
my cold   my consort   my idle
equilibrium   dispossessed

Visions of   formality   a life
glazed over   a misted
landscape   typified
by   haystacks   cloud   the vulnerable
poor   party
to   fabrication   housed
in   a tepee   a shoe   a willow tree

A brook   a plaintive
time of year

The Startle

Peaks & pleats   plummets – now
on the rise again   quickened
as wits may be   forks & tails
turning   tuning
dividing the wider plane – crest
& mantle   loam & sacrifice
O for the moor
the wild & green un-gated life!

Here lies the gist

These yearnings   bent upon
persist . . . wither . . . persist
branches not yet deceased cloven
with false grimaces   particular
& almost plaintive
as the smiles   here placed:
I wish thee lives fluted & fragrant
here lies the jest

Trails behind

Not offering grams or seeds or melons
ripe & gleaming   tired trails
alongside   couching
our wounded selves – encumbered
meek & soft of spine lately
lowered   in swathes
of second best   re-used miscast
spun from doctrines   patchy bits
off shoots   calling themselves
to heel   to flower

Cellophane

Occludes but lightly so

sweet & tensile

a crisp over-thought   clear

& principled   to which a softer meaning

is cast   as with icing sugar

There are times like this when this

is all that's needed a slight dusting

ease of patience

Pick your way mindfully

let governance abide   reeds & rushes

are leaning   the gentle force

swaying   like the bent

of a feather   may touch

If the journey

be a long one

a suitcase   must be sought

of vast proportions   the arduous task

of preparation   does not

come easy   not easy

begun   nor at all   latterly

could be called

disarray   though softly

imposed   folding / smoothing / pressing

down   similar in tonality   liquid

as thought   can be

added to   & added

As pellets pool

& splatter   drip

in the ear   of transfiguration

mellow   & melancholy

& roots are bared   & the spade – the heart

declines to split

in the hush and lull   amidst

the imprecision   the head

ringing like a bell   then the trees

will sway & billow & bend

& the Russian Vine   will wander

not circumspect   like I

Ever so often

At least when sky

is dull slender *sallow / sodden / sullen*

body's weight   heightens

mind's lumbering   lists

slacked words   tilts

recognition   *eyes wonder / eyes booty / eyes reward*

names beauty's slippery

exactness   calls it

lightness   if this be providence

this sustains us

Progress

Were I to be tamed   sufficed

by the odd mention   the occasional

wisp in the cornea   — the perfect place

for an image — though solitary

& unknowing   well then

thy bespoke – nay – homemade

life   as I   would describe

may flail — a somnambulist's

portion   though do not let it

flounder

The inward breath

Once observed   the more consciously

is feigned   nature drifts

below a bridge I am minded to visualise

& I am there & wanting

tho' surprisingly grateful

– the memory (which doesn't exist)

guides   & with the flow

of supposition

a reality takes place

Choose

With scant confidence   cut

the stem of probability   obliquity

the light dips but briefly   assume

an escapade – bring with you

what you will – dynamite

soaked in solitude   no portent

lassitude   nil by intent   This year

the wisteria will be wild   valid

whole racemes   of it

At the end

Gather in the day
up-ended   incomplete
in its ditherings   dull
& unbecoming

Has it anything
to do with you
reinventing its promise
countless times?

Call it – the choice here
is limited – whatever
it matters little
& enormously so

Lest too much be
apportioned to blame   I offer
the minutest of blessings –
may it come your way truly

Expectance

entrances (her) waves

from all directions   as if bells

were peeling   light

overcome with perfume   sweet

lover's touch   were there to be such a one   loft

of all yearning   becomes becoming

discernible   *but it is so!* as landscape

sleeps into darkness   seemingly

not quite there

To one treated as such

The water spider spins a bell like nest
       then fills it with air

Tightly curled   as a lock of hair
an unfurled tulip   a lore
in each cavity   the piercing together
of   what   when   where
&   in what order   *over it blew*
      as were there wind to fumble

A lap-wing   or a diving fish
the back of a head
     brimming
a bole   a steadfast boat
a row of books   already raided
       husk
of the day   that disappeared   rainy
misapprehended

    the water spider spins a bell like nest . . .

Plot

A taker of pains (no sugar)   metallic

wrapped   *sets-out-steps*

blueprint / layout / facsimile   *slender in its eloquence*

jacket ruched with insignia   rain

peeling / pounding   *night-plights nail-bites*

a book for colouring on the open table   *& the tree that sheds its leaves*

repasts of many kinds   *awash with hegemony & ergot*

(visitors of the 18th & 19th centuries are expected any time)

between now & noon calibrates connivers

the next day has away with words   *expectant the weather*

Sweet portfolio!   *seven-rags-to-rich-brides-dish-wives*

settling a part . . . swords at the hem

the mantelpiece realm   *cherry-trove pea-grove birth-pot   thimble*

according to some observers

you are standing on the brim of an alternative

Further on

Beyond the bank   *say-line   fault-loam*

where the bark   cracks

from its hollow core   *grey-spool   hellebore   fistulae*

& sky gathers root   caws & calls   *aye-woe   yaw-way   awe-wry*

light   in its way   overcast   *pheromone   far-fro-ohm*

whispers   *back a bit*   meets

halfway   having forged

then forgot . . .   *two-wit   true-writ   whit-whoa   rune*

skew-schist   skit-a-ling   clew-twist   spill-a-kin
thin-swing   wisp-sting   pen-flick   coil-trick
rick-wrack   cat-snap   tar-tow-tarry   tether & parry

In need of water   forgets

to eat   ears

fit to wander   *ere-fore   err-nor   o'er-nay   nary*   endings

clipped & frayed   *tear & lore   stalk & straw*   stoops

back   steps

her sometime self

In no particular order

At the point where a woman
distanced in time & place seen
to be wearing a pale dress her face
turned to the side her hair fair

The place alarmed

The season becoming spring

The cat dead in the most unpleasant way . . .

It being late & not having eaten

Pens the need

Unexpected quiet in the sky . . .

Select something marvellous:
A gabled roof of the kind a bird will sit upon
in a seaside town (goes some way)
in which one seeks one's fortune Above
an attic window (a car skids / grinds to a halt)
Inside's more of a fog: the end
of a word a coin spun in a well

To make of this

Setting : a detached house   belonging
to an old friend older than her   whose husband
is older still   late & she needs
to get home   Monotone dwellings
she does not recognise   & she
in her Victorian nightdress
can only run on . . .

Endeavour   then it's pouring down
– how fortuitous to meet
an English poet (reads from a weathered volume)
who it just so happens . . .

And what of the gloves that came her way?
dropped discarded   or abandoned
to charity   A seconds thought
hands them over   to one
whose former hand   resembles
that of a werewolf: hair & claws & all

A story of possibility

We're at the point   of shallow glades
still time   no ideas
to whom the bodies belong

A besom swoops twitches   twigs
gainfully tempered
same-here   seem-there   some-whither

Weather coils the cellophane trees
whose rudiments
form   a kind of forest :

Briars trundle   o'er full-bright ridges
– & ferns
fiddlehead / horsetail / obdurate

Trowel & clippers   forage for character
bearing gists & grit
– a squirrel scoots under a car

Simulacra

I minds I moulds . . . melancholia
laps   infringes   the boundary
between states   stealthily it enters
gaining   ground

The pit walls crumble
a house / cliff / garden   succumbs to erosion   tufts
of daisies   daffodil clumps
cease to fulfil
                              reek & havoc

A figure turns a corner   tends your way
one beady eye
                    recedes   resembles   converges

The table is laid for tea
the usual way   escapes tentatively
representation

Something   entirely else
lives underneath   like the girl in the story
grown up   overshadowed
by her former self

From a previous life

Speckle moon – what may you spill?

A rebel of sorts   paints a wishing well

on dry land   *in the middle was a large keep* . . .

Pail   empty as stockings

the morning after   *pain & cinders   fat goose fingers*

Mould   in the cooking pot

gruel in the casket   *there is washing to be done* . . .

Each year   scarcely decorous   *nary nor kilter   riven & splinter*

delivers scant proceedings

Keep us from those   whose knives / playthings / multiples

are stacked   fit to tumble   Clay too

shall wither   *raw ribs & kittens   dry root & brigands*

Such wont such want   such wasn't

Never having seen such lovely flowers

The place is a midden

Various the perspectives   *back-cowl*   *blank-let*   *front-gloom*   *dither*
into which she may blunder   *scatter*   *clutter*   *marrow*

the chairs she may protect   *need-pouch*   *Gretel*   *scuttle & tongs*
preening cushions soothing cloth   *mid-wake*   *cloud-snare*
                                                vale-prune   *natter*

all about her   *bye-gone*   *egg-glade*   *reap-glean*   *garner*
chattels are rising   *freight-flay*   *wound-borne*   *hail-bent*   *blinker*

plumes of scrawny creatures   *pond-stir*   *erst-key*   *spin-tail*   *sparrow*
break & foreclose   *fold-line*   *hip-spur*   *hail-scheme*   *scarper*

seeds of scholarly demise   *sketch-ling*   *scrip-hull*   *ink-bole*   *scrivener*
contain a backlash   *wing-thrip*   *sap-fly*   *gnat-thorn*   *tickler*

Her eye swells   too soon
the seasons end
wither   *hither*   *nether*

Stories

Mistakenly combined   no way
to   recapitulate   so much
foregone

Make a list – a central commotion
around which   fractures
revolve   conclude   set off
repercussions – a dimly lit room   the worst
of the day – drapes
heavily   alluded   *tongs & fender*
something in the air   the ring
of hysteria

Make mine perforated   full
of muted   memorabilia
– small piercings   trinkets   *tricks & tocks*
a walking stick

(Looking neither left nor right
she crosses – makes it
over)

Pod

O *night who doth entreat thee . . .*
A road contiguous to heath land:

brushwood & teasel   spawn-weed & weasel
. . . from which do stars appear

(she) enquires of the nature   inveigles
directions   describes the environ
in the manner of one who lingers
on detail – the precision
of stone   the fey semblance
of shadow

What may it be?

~

The tarmac track:
Inquisitive folk along the way

mud-patch & cross-ditch   pitch-axe & foible
fob-witch yarn-catch bale-switch   dabble . . .

a lowered brow a beggared land

outreached – those rags

have seen wondrous days

rat-a-tat worry-snatch grass-talk twiddle

~

A manner of placing:

One (who) speaks out

quibble-tip tease-trim jest-quip venture
left-brim nestle-brain mind-meld mortar

seems to know her So

repeats her question

underlined & without malice

Arrives at a halt

A thing approaches – maybe a donkey

Here and there are finders

verge-bare scavenge-heap scrip-scree debris

~

A lot happens:

(she) is allotted the task of sweeping up

twinkle little eye (well met)
mirth & mire   sweet & sly   scour the sky   hither & by

without

her cardigan – fine points

maketh the difference – her hair

united in chains of colour

~

O'er the brink of a hillock:

A little picture

calendar – tiny days

& months dangle

~

Corollary:

Through night doth she wonder . . .
pea-case   hornet-husk   shell-pare   sliver

(she) boils beetroot   sweet red beetroot

buries bulbs   bidding

their little shoots

A poem & a bead

Swifts it would be
    under eaves
        around turrets   somewhere
(through an open casement)
            a braided maiden
     On a hillock a fool
in his birthday suit
        hugging his knees

          buddleia
               & antirrhinum
        seeded in the cracks
of parapet walls   a rope ladder
        landing (stealthily)
        over a battlement / a demilune / a rampart / a ravelin

        lower down
          a cart rumbles across cobbles
loses a wheel   a squabble
        ends in fisticuffs apples
            half-red half-green
        are bartered for (anything can be) tossed
           in a barrel Teeth
              rot easily

          An expanse of green
       close cropped (a stage
          would be too small
       though large enough
            for a joust) behind / below
a canopy / arras / awning
        (by no means protective) creeps
        something

human
animal
or of the insect world . . .

a shell (with sails) floats by

under a hedge   a place
for burrowing
(scurry little creature scurry)
a maze of exits
each point each
demarcation
a sallow pattern
paths pagodas   a dove
balanced on a shoulder

a fan of stairs ………….
a ledge of curlicues   a cooling
glass of sherbet
on a ceremonial salver
a tinder box
a banished lover

floats to the water's edge

a lattice fence
a fretted border   a bridge
to a distant land
its cargo   a poem & a bead

There are fireworks about
they splay & squander
in the afterlife
a small suggestion
like the tips
of leaves

There is little tonight for supper

Widen where the days fall
familiar feeds the kettle

Bread needs the tin of strife
barely grows the scuttle

Wind-spill window's ill
copper-mould & pickled-pill

Null till the frame's bled
wilder than the racket

Sun-shrugs barley-lugs
pig rings & pellets

Sip-sluice the wicker dregs
trip-trap the bucket

Tooth-rind slop-drill
life-blag & gullet

One-two the skillet shed
shoo-shod the robber sped

Chaff-pinch hearth's lead
treacle mince & stuffing

Stock still the ricket bed
bolder than the rabbit

Pot-thrust dust-spread
cold-sprouts & rat's head

O blessed rags

seeped in fervour

larded up with heather

Mallow-May

Mellow may   loop of the spool   seed
of the caraway   soup
for the mule

Calumny calumny   stake
of complacency   Tapestry fallacy   fable
of infancy

Tassel-tree   nether-bee   stave
of democracy
derring-do   derring-do   (secret isocracy)

Scholar of infamy   Pitcher of fantasy
Printer of destiny   Tenant of cool

Sing to me   Sing to me
kettle & timpani
roundelay   ricochet
scatter & rule

The reading

A plastic chair – *take me rest your feet*
– a broken bench (she arranges the seating)

She can't read (tries to) what is
*un*written no longer words   not even

between the lines All the elements are there
– like floaters in the eye hard

to pin down – *stay still* while I make you out!
Small hills rise & fall Ah! – a road a lane

narrowing tumbledown a gatepost a vestibule – almost
a way in This one curves negligently   its little tail

probing (she used to know what that meant)
What is it like to lose a mind – or never to know

it is missing? A route map of liquid thought – before
thought coheres congeals A tongue thick

with mystification *Think* – round the edges
over the top (of spectacles?) right to left

laterally Diagonalise (how a word search
can catch you out) All that is sat upon

rises to the surface Be reassured
On this day (of mists and mildews) the path

begins benignly The trick
is to know it's there Verily it is

The audience faces away – she is speaking
to the backs of heads . . .

Transcribe transliterate: a version
writes itself – pictographic historiated Follow

with your finger – as you go along
invent the words

a pit   a gloom   a stage   a knot

a nail   a zoom   a twitch   a block

a schism   a stool   a wield   a frock

a sweet   a swirl   a side   a lock

twice thrown   first sewn   a bean   a sock

prize & passion   field & chasm

button   boulder   bale & billet

cake & sham   quail & fillet

sense of sparrow   flick of rhythm

time's vest   snail quest

din & quibble   lace & nest

make more over   pick more clover

cook & grumble   hail life's bundle

Lightning Source UK Ltd.
Milton Keynes UK
UKOW03f0314260417
299885UK00002B/121/P